"To Change a Nation"

By Juliet Dawn

3

All poetry written by Juliet Dawn
~inspired by the Holy Spirit

Artwork by Lizzie Westhead
(who sadly went to be with the Lord in 2010)

Produced and designed by Juliet Dawn

Published by Dovetail Music
www.dovetail~music.co.uk

Endorsements

"Juliet Dawn's poetry has been birthed in the fire of God's jealous love and broken heart for His people - both in Britain and Israel. There is a cry of anguish, but also faith. Juliet's tear-stained poetry represents a breakthrough in the great legacy of British psalmistry. May these powerful poems touch and change many hearts.!
David Davis - Founder/Senior Pastor Carmel Assembly, Haifa, Israel

"These are poems for our time. Juliet Dawn has a highly unusual and creative anointing to bring the heart of God in unique and striking verse which will touch your soul, speak to your spirit and inspire you to awake, arise and take your place."
Judy Littler Manners, Fountain House - National Strategic Co-ordinator

"Using her God given prophetic talent, in this book, Juliet Dawn has delivered a heartfelt cry from Heaven. Prepare to be encouraged, inspired, challenged and stirred as you read through this selection of poems that call for understanding and action in regard to God's passion for the Nations. I highly recommend this work."
Rev. Steve Mullins Dip.Th -Evangelist - Dry Bones Trust

"I am delighted and honoured to write this endorsement as I believe that in these prophetic poems Juliet has captured and expressed the heart of God for the nation. I also truly believe that they have the power to change a nation, our nation and nations if we will heed what God is saying through them.
Thank you Juliet for being obedient to His leading. God bless you."
Dr. Anne Rowntree - National Intercessor and Prayer Warrior

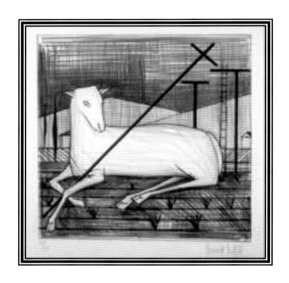

"...and of the increase of His Government and peace,
there shall be no end." Isaiah ch 9 v 7

Foreword

This book of poems has been born out of an ever increasing desire to bring the call of destiny to the church and God's Kingdom. In these significant, sobering and worrying times, my ear has been intent on listening to what God would say to His people to bring them into maturity and a clear understanding of the prophetic days in which we live. I am as certain as any person can be that God's end time agenda includes (and even centre's around) Israel and the Jewish people and therefore, this too is reflected in the content of this book.

Several years ago, God gave me a commission to share His heart, and in obedience, that is what this book aims to address—it is not about poetry, but about the cry and call of God to His Church. The cumulative effect is to hopefully bring a deepening sense of urgency to anyone who seeks to live righteously before God and facilitate His purposes and plans as we serve Him in the preparation of His coming Kingdom.

I pray that you will read this with an open heart, an open mind and an open spirit so that the cry of God's heart can impact on you greatly and spur you on to make life changing decisions and be significant for Christ!

Be bold, be courageous and be responsive..... this is not a book you read passively! Share with friends, prayer partners and groups..... let's change the nation AND the nations (if we dare believe we can)‼ Psalm 2 v 8

Contents

Gone Too Far p.12
A plea to our Father regarding our Godless lands

Holy Fire p.14
Revelation regarding the coming fire and its purpose

My Israel... p.18
God's declaration of promise and destiny for Israel

One New Man p.22
Truths regarding the Church's Hebraic heritage and future

God of the Breakthrough p.26
God's reminder that in world crisis, He is still God and is still in control

Every Second Matters p.30
A timely warning of how close we are to the climax of biblical prophecy

What in the World... p.32
God's outpouring of disappointment at the offence He sees in the Church

The Militant Bride p.34
War cry! Strategy! Enemy briefing! Call to Arise!

To Break the Chains of Darkness p.40
An inspiring prayer & declaration of sovereignty over our nation

Oh God Forgive Us! p.42
Collective repentance on behalf of Europe for our treatment of Israel

Fury Rises! p.48
A stark warning from God regarding His coming wrath concerning Israel

State of the Nation p.52
A call to the Church to see and understand the signs of the times

Arise! p. 54
A call from God for a practical response in ratifying His Holy alignments

Contacts and Resources p.60 - 62

WARNING:
This book could seriously and permanently
change your thought-life and increase your
prayer life - you have been warned!!

Gone Too Far!

Oh Lord, our hearts are sodden with grief,
For this Godless land of unbelief,
As every right has turned to wrong,
We've stayed our foot and held our tongue.

    Every wicked way and immoral act,
    Unrighteous law and sinful pact,
    Has slipped our watch, through blatant gaps,
    As we've guarded Your name with shameful lapse.

Oh Lord, our eyes are stinging with tears;
We've defaced Your earth, through arrogant years:
We've abused the soil and polluted the air,
With barely a flinch and hardly a care.

    Every tree we've felled , and creature slain,
    Every species warped and global stain,
    Has gone unchecked as we've blinked and smiled,
    And played at church as the world is defiled.

Oh Lord, our hands are smeared with guilt,
For we've crippled the chosen nation You built.
The Israel You made and divinely preserved,
Was cruelly betrayed, with spite undeserved.

    Every cry for help and desperate plea,
    Met only hate-fuelled apathy.
    We locked the Jews into genocide,
    And turned our backs as millions died!

Oh Lord, our spirits are aching with shame,
For we stood in the wings as they banished Your name:
This Christian land, that once You prized,
Has been shared with Islam, and secularised.

Every bible replaced and cross torn down,
Has stolen a jewel from Your holy crown:
Every tenet repealed, as your people stood dumb,
Has made us the feeble church we've become.

So Lord, our bones are rigid with fear,
For its gone way beyond any path we can steer,
We're embarrassed and helpless; undone by despair,
And we're turning to You in united prayer.

You know Your church; though ruptured and weak:
You know the cries we're unable to speak:
So Father God, as we come to our knees,
Forgive us, and heal our nation; please!

Juliet Dawn

"...feeble church"

13

I See Your Holy Fire!

"Written in March 2007 in response to a dancing vision that came in the periphery of my vision - when I asked God what it was... He said it was His Holy Fire!"

I see the dancing shadow of Your Holy Fire.
It sits on the periphery of my vision.
It flickers with all the authority of heaven and beckons to my quizzical flesh and hungry spirit.
But what is this Holy Fire?
Where, how and on what will it fall?
Its flame beats with power and intensity, threatening to unleash itself with unstoppable purpose.
But what is this Holy Fire? Oh God, what is this Holy Fire?

Could it be the promised empowerment of Christendom?
Is it the Holy Fire of old, re-kindled to inject fearsome enabling into a weary church?
Is it the answer to prayer for revival, for the miraculous and for the awesome signs and wonders that are worthy of our King?
Is it a physical form of Your Spirit's power, wielding the full weight of its incredible and infinite possibilities?
  ◦ Is it knocking on God's prophetic door, impatient to fulfil destiny?
  ◦ Is it eagerly waiting for its moment in the final chapter of time?
I wonder... is *this* what's waiting in the wings of the earth's stage?

"It is coming.."

Could it be Your wrath, Oh God, crackling with the fury of Your breath?
Is it Your judgement, Oh Father, on stubborn mankind that has slandered Your name, embraced evil and deceived its offspring?
Is it the destruction of which You have warned, that will consume Your enemies and unmercifully destroy that which stands in the way of Your decrees?
Is it the execution of Your spoken Word that has ordained divine and eternal consequences for those that have conspired against Your heavenly mandate?
 ○ Is it perfecting its deadly intent as it awaits Your very command?
 ○ Is it surveying its prey as the heat intensifies?
I wonder... is *this* the stirring of Your retribution ignited after years of restraint despite persistent rebellion?

Could it be the rescue plan for Your ancient home, Jerusalem?

Is it the weaponry of Your long established promise to reclaim Zion for Your chosen nation?

Is it bound to blaze through every blasphemous temple that has desecrated the soul and landscape of Your Holy City?

Is it the instrument by which the world will witness the humiliation, wounding and eventual defeat of Your adversary in the final battle for Christ's landing strip?

- Is it rehearsing its centre stage performance in the pages of history?
- Is it gathering ferocity as it waits?

I wonder... is *this* Your Holy armoury; stoked, prepared and ready to strike in the most strategic combat of all time?

Or, could it be all of these, Oh God?

Is the unsuspecting world about to experience a fragment of Your might?

Is humanity about to encounter the God of biblical yesteryear, who displayed His hand without concealment or detachment?

Or, is the fire in abeyance, awaiting our response before knowing its own destiny?

Is it waiting for its Master's voice?

I see Your Holy Fire.
It sits on the periphery of my vision.
What is this Holy Fire, Oh God?
Without hesitation, one thing is certain....
it is coming, it is coming soon!

Juliet Dawn

MY ISRAEL

Israel, oh Israel, My people, My land,
Long have I wept for each purpose I planned,
For kingship, glory, honour and power,
But now is your time; now is your hour!

I promised your forefathers long ago,
That I'd never forsake you, nor let you go,
That I'd favour your sons and prosper your nation,
That I'd honour your race with the gift of salvation.

I haven't abandoned each promise I made.
You *are* still My chosen, though lost and afraid.
You've been crushed and downtrodden and set apart
..and its burned in My spirit and broken My heart.

I've seen you abused; I've followed your plight;
Each battle, each war, each murder, each fight,
But I allowed it to happen as you turned your own way,
And I've watched and I've waited in grief and dismay.

You rejected My grace, My protection, My favour;
You rejected My son, Yeshua, your Saviour,
And though I am wounded through want of your love,
I've etched your destiny, in the Heavens above.

"...now is your time"

But the light is now coming; a new day will dawn.
No longer, your God will weep and mourn.
I'm raising an army, both strong and bold,
To bring to pass all the prophets foretold.

I've awakened My people to see through My eyes,
The injustice you've suffered, the generations of lies.
So as warriors in Christ, they've partnered your cause;
Your fight is now theirs and theirs will be yours.

They are clothed in the truth, knowing all that's to come.
They're your family in Christ: in My name, you're one.
I've called them as watchmen, to earnestly pray,
So see what they see and hear what they say.

New life grafted in to the old olive tree
(Yes) Your strength will come in unity.
So see how these branches have come to your aid.
Don't be suspicious! Don't be afraid!

I'm calling you back to that which you own.
Zion is beckoning, go back to your home.
The darkness is lifting, I'm unveiling your eyes.
It's (your) time Jerusalem. Arise! ..Arise!

"...the darkness is lifting..."

Each prophecy stands, divinely appointed
To restore you to Me, My brave and anointed.
I will bless those who bless you, I will curse those who curse.
My word won't be void: not a breath, not a verse!

And so it is in these final days,
As the world looks on through a slumberous haze,
My church in all nations will heed the call,
And turn their heads to your holy walls.

Through their spiritual warfare, outrage and pity,
I will keep My vow and give you your city,
For it's not just your birthright, it's also My will
'Cause the Lord's feet will land there, on Olivet's Hill.

So Israel, oh Israel, My people, My land,
As confusion recedes, I call you to stand,
Alongside your brothers, as I wait for your cry,
"Baruch Ha Ba Be'shem Adonai!"

"Blessed is He that comes in the name of the Lord!"

Juliet Dawn

"...turn their heads to your Holy walls"

"Written in 2005 shortly after the death of my twin boys - I look back now and realise that God stayed my hand in the writing of this and only allowed it to come forth in my grief, thus aligning with His own broken heart!"

One New Man

Echad, Echad, One New Man!
The pivotal key of God's awesome plan.
The seed that He laid and the offspring that grew,
Is the "trampled-on" truth of the Gentile and Jew.

Though many disown any family ties,
Having fed from the poison of decades of lies,
This sibling and kin, share the same DNA,
For the root has not changed with the years of decay.

God sowed the foundation through one man assigned,
Abraham's line would bless all of mankind,
An' through Isaac and Jacob, God's Kingdom was earthed,
And the truth was declared as His nation was birthed.

Yet Israel was lawless and wilful and weak,
And they fooled themselves blind, with much arrogant speak,
'Til they spurned their Messiah and sent Him to death,
'Though He sought to forgive, with His last dying breath.

From the dregs of this "Faith" as God veiled their eyes,
A new style of church would emerge and arise,
But feeling self-proud as their knowledge increased,
They berated the Jews and abandoned their feasts!

Yes, Christianity hijacked the Church,
And the Hebrew traditions were snubbed and besmirched,
The name of the Father was stripped and defaced,
As the Hebraic, Yahweh.... was duly replaced!

Yeshua was shelved to its old Jewish perch,
With *Jesus the Saviour*, now Head of the Church,
And flags and symbols, traditions and tribes,
Were promptly dispensed with the Torah and Scribes.

Yet here we are, many centuries on,
The wounds are still raw and the hatred's not gone,
BUT, God's healing balm is decanted and stirred,
To be poured on his promises, etched in His Word.

With jealously roused by the Gentile's praise,
The veil will be lifted from Israel's gaze:
The dry bones WILL live, as they rise to God's schemes,
And they'll see their Messiah in visions and dreams.

And as the world stoops to the treacherous brink,
God's Gentile and Jew will be ushered to link,
And united in Christ they'll be valiant and strong
Both now sapping the root to which they belong.

"Christianity hijacked the Church..."

United in Christ, United in truth,
Naomi now drawn to the goodness of Ruth,
Mara diminished, all bitterness crushed,
For the enmity's lost as Her heart has been touched!

The faiths are entwining; One God at the fore.
The Lion of Judah restored now to roar,
And call all His children to ultimate war:
Two people; One purpose; God's truth at its core!!

Echad, Echad, One New Man!
The pivotal key of God's awesome plan.
Spirits combine and the army unites...
As the power of Yeshua, inspires and ignites.

Echad, Echad, ~ a New Man bold!
Beware the world as this force will unfold!
Christians and Israel, now jointly Christ's own,
Will rule with the King, as the Lord takes His throne!!

Juliet Dawn

"...United in Christ"

I know that your hearts here are heavy,
I know that you're troubled in mind,
I know there's more questions than answers,
And I know that these days are unkind.

I know you have lost those you cherish,
I know that you're hurt and confused
I know that your prayers grow impatient
And I know that your faith has been bruised.

I know that you're tired of your worries,
I know that you're desperate for peace,
I know that your bodies are weary,
And I know that your battles increase.

I know that your families are shaken,
I know that your strength has been sapped,
I know that you see much to fear,
And I know that so many feel trapped.

BUT, I am the Lord God of Israel,
Your Mighty, Victorious King,
And I will not ever desert you,
For I cradle you under My wing.

I know life has treated you cruelly,
I know that the season is black,
I know that My church feels frustrated,
For it seems there is nothing but lack.

BUT, I am your Father in Heaven,
And all that you see I have made,
I know the end and beginning,
So My Bride, you should not be afraid.

I call you to hold your faith tightly,
I call you to lay its roots deep,
Just cling to the rock that is Jesus,
And look to My face as you weep.

I weep with you also, for Israel,
Their plight has provoked Me to act,
So your time and their time have junctured,
And tell all your leaders this fact!

Yes, all around you may crumble,
The earth may be rocked to its core,
The world may collapse under crisis,
And nations speak murder and war.

"..hold your faith tightly"

BUT, do not give up 'midst disaster,
Be not despondent and weak,
Lay down confusion and trembling,
Surrender your doubt as I speak!

I am the GOD OF THE BREAKTHROUGH,
I have My all-conquering plan,
I'm depending on you to out-play it,
And that's why this test is on man.

Stand on My Word and keep righteous,
Be most alert in this hour,
This time of great trial and struggle,
Has shown Me My army of power.

I am the Omega and Alpha,
So hear this as strength to your soul,
I will make a way in the darkness,
I Am still the God in control!

Juliet Dawn

Light through the dark

Every Second Matters....

Every second matters,
Every minute counts,
Life is slowly ticking by in God's pre-planned amounts.

The days are breathing heavy,
They splutter and they lurch,
The end of time is clear in sight, and we're asleep, Oh church!

The hours now are numbered,
The years remain but few,
Has yet the sense of urgency, to full descend on you?

God's given out His warnings,
By prophet, hand and pen,
He long foretold the crucial signs of how and what and when.

Beware the age is waning,
It's later than you think,
The anti-Christ will claim his throne before the world can blink!

Players are positioned,
Prophecies are lined,
We're living end-time scripture, yet we act as though we're blind

Bible views we elbow,
And Godly ways we mock,
It's edging close to midnight now on God's prophetic clock!

"Written in March 2009, inspired and stirred by prophetic words and inspired teaching."

Yes, every word now matters,
Each decision counts,
Life is slowly ticking by, as fast the darkness mounts...

Juliet Dawn

"...edging close to midnight"

What In The World Are You Doing....

What in the world am I seeing, My church?
As My eyes wander over My flock,
Some have lost hold,
Of how days will unfold,
And it seems that My ways they would mock!

What in the world are you doing? I ask,
As the last years of time are in view,
You gossip with hate,
You judge and berate,
More concerned with what others would do.

What in the world are you hearing? I ask,
While My prophets speak clear of these times,
You delight in the sin,
Of your brother and kin,
And waste breath assessing their crimes.

What in the world is your focus? I ask,
While parliament strangles your rights,
Your hearts are consumed,
With offence you have groomed,
And grievance lies full in your sights.

What in the world are you thinking? I ask,
While the enemy steps up his game,
Your bitterest thoughts
And indignant retorts,
Will render you spiritually lame.

Forgiveness...

What in the world is your purpose? I ask,
As I share of the plans for My bride,
Your heart and your gaze,
Fix on man's errant ways,
And your conflicts just gird up your pride.

What in the world are you speaking? I ask,
As I call you to holier ways,
Your unrighteous tongues,
In recounting or wrongs,
Will tarnish these critical days.

What in the world is important? I ask,
As the world sets its stage for the end,
Will you learn to forgive,
...and choose love as you live,
Or continue your feud with your friend?

What in the world can I tell you? I ask,
Your quarrelling saddens me deep,
Will intolerance wane,
As my purposes reign?
Will you look to your shepherd, My sheep?

What in the world is accomplished, you ask,
By sharing My heart for so few?
Let the Spirit convict,
Where a conscience is pricked,
Just maybe these words are for you?!

Juliet Dawn

"Written in 2009, directly inspired by a teaching series by
Brenda Taylor called "What in the World is happening?".
I really felt the pull of God's aching heart on this!"

THE MILITANT BRIDE

Wake up! Oh Church, My army, My bride,
To all who will listen, My Kingdom wide,
I summon all troops to My war counsel suite,
Awake from your beds! Come out of retreat!

The enemy plots, conspires and spies,
With rare intent he conjures up lies,
Which, black with scorn, he weaves to his plan,
To cripple the Church and subjugate man.

With blood red ink he draws-up his schemes,
To suffocate hope and shatter all dreams,
He never takes rest in his ruthless pursuit,
For his selfish desires lie deep at its root.

Beware, oh Church, for in swift, steady flow,
His demons are briefed with new evil to sow,
Then promptly, released, on their wicked crusade,
Equipped to divide and to pillage and raid!

But see, not just demons advance to the field,
For many a pawn is now fatally sealed,
To wrangle control, for the prince of the air
And he plays them like dice as they work, unaware.

"Wake up!"

"...come out of retreat"

Governments, bankers, Heads of States,
Gurus, Lords and magistrates,
Are smeared with stains and seem to drip,
With ink red prints from Satan's grip.

Yet, here is your strongest, sharpest foe;
As the counterfeit church continues to grow,
Religions and cults with political slants,
Pervade all your statutes: surround you like ants!

Prophets of peace peddling ear-pleasing views,
Teachers of wisdom who softly confuse,
Mongers of hate who speak terror and war,
Despotic dictators who make their own law.

Many speak cunning, so hard to detect,
Eloquent speeches, commanding respect.
But do not be blind, for concealed in their hands,
Is a hell-devised mandate to steal your lands.

Yes, enemies scuttle in chambers of power,
Their well-rehearsed statements, well-placed for the hour,
And welcomed, accepted, they're staking their claim,
On all that your kinsmen fought bravely to gain.

Close not your eyes, to the threat of attack,
Around ev'ry corner and deep in each crack,
Evil contrives to bring poison to bear,
And it's time to be ready! It's time to prepare!

So, let go your comfortable, pew-sitting stance,
It's way past the time for religious romance!
This isn't just war; it's the ultimate fight,
For the pace has stepped up as the end is in sight!

So listen My Church, there's so much at stake!
We meet under siege to unite and awake,
It's not propaganda: the battle is drawn!
We're here at the season for which you were born!

The words I have spoken could not be more stark,
They're strong and compelling to dissipate dark,
So look to My Spirit and know you won't fail,
'Gainst hell's fiercest forces, My Bride *will* prevail.

Only a few will respond to My call,
But do not despair that your numbers are small,
Like Gideon's army, your victory's assured.
Remember, the battle belongs to the Lord!

"stand up and take courage"

"Arise! and shine!"

So children of valour, I'm leading your ranks,
I'm mindfully stocking your weaponry banks,
I'm gifting each one with new heavenly skill,
To claim the high ground and accomplish My will.

Don't build a fortress defending your light,
Arise! and shine! Make show of My might,
Advance to all camps in battalion stride,
Resuscitate life where My truth has but died.

Campaign and protest with unstoppable cause,
Do not take sleep as they plunder your shores,
Seek not just freedom, but passion and soul,
To proudly take back what the enemy stole!

Stand up and take courage, do not hold back!
Speak out My Word to launch bullets and flack,
Enlist warring angels in chariots on high,
Let "Jesus is King!" be your militant cry.

Warriors and watchmen, - engage, hand in hand!
Be wise and resourceful and spy out the land,
Strategise Generals! Outwit and outsmart!
But shield out contempt and keep righteous your heart.

So stay ever closer, be near Me and pray,
My fire will protect you: do not go astray!
I'm asking endurance, to strike and defend;
I'm looking for those who'll defy and contend.

It will not be easy, but hearken My voice,
It's do or it's die, and there's really no choice!
The dark is advancing with merciless zeal,
And is fast on your tail and hard at your heel.

So look to your King, your Captain of Hosts,
Return with My sword and attend to your posts,
Put on My armour that cannot be breached
And urgently tend to a world not yet reached.

Blast on the trumpet and beat out My drum!
- Tremble, oh earth, as My foot soldiers come -
Lift up your banners and raise up a shout,
Then awesome! resplendent! and fearless! - march out!

Juliet Dawn

"..defy and contend"

"Written in 2008 under a strong and tangible anointing that grew over several weeks in listening to powerful teachers and prophetic words from heaven during meetings"

... TO BREAK THE CHAINS OF DARKNESS

"Written for the London "Israel Key to UK Revival" conference in February '10
God gave a very clear vision of the spiritual strategy and from here,
this strong message to the conference emerged."

Here in this Land of Greatness, a shred of hope remains,
That all will not be harnessed by the darkness and its reins.
Though lies have grown like fungus, and spores have spread to power,
This age of flagrant unbelief has not foreseen this hour.

We see the nation smitten; in love with just herself;
She cannot see her blackness; just nobility and wealth.
Yet, vapours of foul discourse, permeate the air,
And equal rights and liberal views, deflect all moral glare.

Shrivelled veins of decency lie strangled by the tether
Of the one world propaganda, that all faiths can work together.
All moral fibre rubbished, all truths are trimmed and clipped,
The Godly laws marked "out of date", are shredded, binned and snippe

The chains of darkness rattle, for ears that hear the times,
And the jangle of the shackles, ring out all human crimes.
The stealth that partnered Babel, now reaches for this snare,
To tighten and embroil; to fasten and impair!!

But stealth has not accounted for the remnant and the few,
Who see the global trappings... and know just what to do.
They've listened to God's warnings; they've agreed and understood,
That any plot of Satan's can be broken by the blood!

They've come to meet for business and to terrify the skies,
With Messiah's name victorious as proclamations rise.
They'll raise a cry to Heaven, that penetrates its walls,
And summons Heaven's armies, as God's mighty power falls.

It breaches hell's defences and it draws God's mercy down,
It stirs prophetic purpose and it brings the King to town.
God's awesome might discerns it, and He stoops to catch the pain,
Of a host of voices praying, that deception WILL NOT REIGN!

Let here, the Kingdom's battle! Let here our God descend!
To usher Heaven's purpose for the lands that we defend.
Release the Lion of Judah, with a loud majestic roar,
And let the strongholds quiver, for He'll crush them in His jaw!

His name be high exalted, by the passion of His Bride,
As Jew and Gentile praise Him, united side by side.
The cry that hits the throne room will woo the Lion's sword,
With ascending faith and worship and our hearts in one accord.

The chains that hold the nation, can be smashed with Yahweh's plan,
It's God; His power and mercy, and the cries of "one new man"!
Symbolic, we can conquer, as we wield the Lion's might,
And declare the blood of Jesus, in this history- changing fight.

We pray for mercy Father, in this settling of accounts,
We pledge our love for Israel in immeasurable amounts,
We hail you Righteous Victor and we pray Your presence speed,
To obliterate the darkness in this very present need.

Let here it be recorded! Let here it be declared!
That we, Your Kingdom people, are faithfully prepared;
We'll pray and we will battle, on fire with passion's flame...
'Til strongholds crack and wither, 'neath the power of Your name!

Let here, the Kingdom's battle! Let here our God descend!
To usher Heaven's purpose for the lands that we defend.
Release the Lion of Judah! Let His government increase!
May He Break the chains of darkness…. and His Kingdom never cease!

Juliet Dawn

OH GOD FORGIVE US !

Today is time for exposure :
Today the truth will reign.
For this God-ordained assembly,
Will not convene in vain.

Its not just the usual business :
Its not just the Church in its stride.
We declare this is destiny changing,
For You`ve ear-marked this day for Your Bride !

Oh God let our hearts be so humbled !
Oh God let our spirits align,
With every decree You have purposed,
As the prayers of Your people combine.

(Oh God Forgive us !)

How abhorrent here before You !
How abhorrent in Your sight,
How we, collective Europe,
Compounded Israel`s plight !

We`ve dressed ourself as honest :
We`ve dressed ourself as pure,
But Europe once so noble,
Is now the devil's whore !

We`ve sold ourself to power :
We`ve sold ourself to greed :
We`ve fed on lies of Islam,
And defied what You`ve decreed !`

"..this is destiny changing"

42

(Oh God Forgive us!)

We`ve broken holy mandates:
We`ve broken binding pacts.
We`ve sold the Jews to slaughter,
And then compromised the facts!

We took back land You`d given:
We took reserves of gold.
We`ve stolen Israel`s finance,
And it wasn`t ours to hold!

We sanctioned unjust treaties:
We sanctioned unjust force.
We`ve worked to quash Your people,
In ways we still endorse!

(Oh God Forgive Us!)

Through hist'ry we have tortured:
Through hist'ry there is shame:
Through years of Inquisition,
We murdered in Your name!

There`s blood spilled throughout Europe.
There`s blood spilled by our hand.
And the lost cries of Your people,
Still echo through these lands!

There`s brutal execution:
There`s brutal, senseless crime!
We`ve victimised Your chosen,
And the horrors stretch through time!

(Oh God Forgive Us!)

What sins have blackened Europe!
What sins have brought Your curse!
But Lord we ask for mercy,
As we seek to bring reverse.

How compelling our offences!
How compelling is our guilt!
But Lord we ask forgiveness,
For this Babel we have built!

How wrong is Europe's footing!
How wrong is Europe's aim!
But Lord we say we're sorry,
As in lieu, we take the blame.

It`s not too late for changes!
It's not too late for shift!
Can we re-anchor Europe
Where she`s badly come adrift?

We dare to pray Your favour,
We dare to pray Your grace,
We're strong in our agreement,
That we move from our disgrace!

It`s time for declaration!
It`s time to claim back ground!
We`ll fill the skies of Europe....
Let the praying church resound!

"...time to claim back ground"

"..not hushed by men"

We are not thwart by government!
We are not hushed by men!
But God we trust Your Lordship,
Let Your mandate rise again!

We declare assignments cancelled!
We declare our captor void!
In Your name Lord we proffer
That hell`s mandate be destroyed!

Release the needed finance Lord!
Release the needed power;
That strategies confound the foe,
In this decisive hour!

(Oh God Forgive Us!)

Accounts now must be settled:
Accounts now must be squared.
Is there a chance oh Father,
That Europe may be spared?
Betrayal of Your people!
Betrayal of Your laws!
We stand accused on all counts, Lord
With just and valid cause.

She`s spiritually listless:
She`s spiritually weak:
She's raped by anti-semites,
And she's found no voice to speak!

(Oh God Forgive Us!)

Let the Church rise up in protest!
Let the Church become your voice!
May "one new man " in victory,
Give Europe back her choice!

Repentance meets with wisdom :
Repentance meets with prayer,
To call a Kingdom onslaught,
To redeem, respond, repair!

It's business <u>not</u> as usual ;
It's business Kingdom born!
Our cries must touch the heavens,
If a new day is to dawn.

(Oh God Forgive Us!)

May Europe see clear her folly!
May Europe dismount the beast!
May shackles that tie her to Islam,
Be fully and ever released!

Oh God! May Joel`s army,
Effect a political sway.
May destiny be uprooted,
And placed in Your hands we pray!

May divine intervention be actioned :
Foundations be shaken on earth!
We`re Blowing the Trumpet in Zion,
Let a new Europa be birthed!!

Juliet Dawn

"... a new Europa be birthed"

"Written in Geneva in May 2010 in my hotel room. We were in Geneva for the ground breaking conference "European Day of Repentance" which aimed to address before God our ill-treatment of the Jewish people."

FURY RISES!

This cause is not a pastime, a fantasy or game!
Look and see My Israel! Lost and weak and lame!
You think I'm not impassioned as I see My cherished flail?
The world has filtered vision; seeing all through Islam's veil.

Hatred meets with poison, and poison turns to war:
No ally left for Israel, she's accused on every score.
But you have heard My warnings; My Bride should know the trut
An' it's time to heed My calling, for Naomi needs her Ruth.

Respond this day with action and passion in your heart.
You're meant to bear My purposes, be bold and set apart!
But Church has carried apathy and edited My Word,
So caught up in religion, that My voice has not been heard!

Yet you are those My people who have caught My Spirit's cry.
I'm aching for My Chosen, as their enemies will try
To crush them and destroy them and make the world believe,
That somehow they're deserving of the onslaught they receive!

This is VILE injustice and it makes My anger rise!
And you who are the gentiles, should not absorb these lies!
My ancient words are standing and will not be overthrown,
That Zion is My Glory and her people are My own!

"..be bold and set apart!"

So hear My children! Listen! For the time grows ever near,
When enemies of Israel will be crippled by their fear,
For I WILL unleash My fury and exercise My Might,
As all that stands against her, will be judged and then be smite!

Do not be left uncertain of the things that are to come.
My rule will be established from My throne, Jerusalem!
And powers, lands and nations, that stand to thwart this plan,
Will taste the wrath of Heaven, as My armies meet with man!

Yahweh stands with Israel; believe that it is so!
The hands that strangle Israel are also Heaven's foe.
Yes, Scripture bears My promises; they're there for all to find,
The years have not erased them - just the Church is largely blind!

Align yourself with Israel, for she needs your watchful prayer.
The threat of mass destruction lingers daily in the air!
I'm making clear My purpose, so you won't mis-hear My will...
She is evermore My Chosen and her torment grieves Me still!

Escalate your mission! Escalate your prayer!
Escalate your purpose! Demonstrate you care!
The bombs may breach the boundaries, - but so do all your cries,
And they're merging over Zion, as My judgement fills the skies!

Juliet Dawn

49

"...My judgement fills the skies"

"Written on October 9th 2010 on the eve of the Welsh National Day of Repentance -"Israel, Key to UK Revival". At dinner that night I had been dramatically impacted by stories of Israel's plight and how God was surely feeling about world events and the church's response" 50

Notes / Personal Prayer

"Written on 27th November 2010 in the van on the way to Westminster for the "State of the Nation" event."

Consider the state of the nation,
...and what a state she is in! ...
By any assessment or measure,
She's totally servant to sin.

It isn't a question of viewpoint,
Perspective, opinion or sway:
This nation has fallen from" greatness",
And is rotten with Godless decay!

Yes, Islam has wrangled and pressured,
And Britain has bowed to her force,
But MORE than this anti-Christ torrent,
Has blown the UK of her course!

We've legalised same sex marriage!
We've said it's OK to abort!
We've turned a blind eye to corruption,
..... as long as you don't get caught!

BUT, God took His hand off our nation,
When *we* took our eyes off the Jews,
For when you betray Yahweh's chosen,
There's no doubt about it – you'll lose!!

SO... good thing we've gathered together,
For God has some plans up His sleeve!
Our prayers and our spirit-filled worship,
Can prosper a judgement reprieve!

Relentless, we'll worship Messiah,
And break through the spiritual mess,
And Lord will release heaven's angels,
To clean up the filth and the cess!

"...the dross is already ignited"

They'll come with the keys to the Kingdom,
To unlock the doors and the gates,
That will release power and blessing,
And truth that will silence debates!

The truth will establish like fire,
For every heart that would thirst,
Burning up lies and deception....
And starting in Christendom first!

It's truth that will banish our weakness;
God's secrets the strength to our prayer,
With angels directing our wisdom,
And showing us how to prepare.

The tide is assuredly turning,
God's face resting full on His church,
For this remnant who've earnestly sought him,
Have captured His heart in His search.

So much is now resting upon us,
To capture the truth in the flames:
The dross is already ignited,
And Christ is re-stating HIs claims.

United we'll strengthen and conquer!
With keys we will unlock the doors!
With truth we will banish deception!
.... for God has stepped in to our cause!

DO NOT rest your eyes in this moment!
DO NOT fall asleep at this hour!
We are stood on the cusp of a judgement,
And the ultimate release of God's power!

See! Hear! Unite! Respond! Prepare!

Juliet Dawn

ARISE !

The strategies are imparted,
The foundations have been laid,
The end-time script has started,
As covenants have been made.
My mandate has been driven,
As plans have been revealed,
Commissions have been given,
And vows here have been SEALED.

Your alignment lies with Israel,
Your passion must increase,
Your courage must not fail,
And your warfare must not cease.
The preparation has lingered,
The understanding is clear,
The enemy's ploys have been fingered,
And My retribution is near.

So listen now as encouragement and instruction.

Your nations have been shaken,
Your spirits have been stirred,
Your voices have been taken,
But your hearts are undeterred.
You've cried and I've cried with you,
I've called and you've obeyed,
You've prayed that I forgive you,
And judgement has been stayed....

"your passion must increase.."

"Written 3rd February 2011 on the eve of
"Israel - Key to UK Revival" conference weekend."

"... I urge you to arise!"

I've warned and you've paid heedance,
You've knelt and called My name,
You've given Israel credence,
As prayers dispel her shame.
You've bravely fought opinion,
You've spoken out My Word,
You've serviced truth's dominion,
As the lies have now been blurred.

You've wooed My full attention,
You've bid My presence come,
And Heaven's heard each mention
Of Messiah, King, My Son!
I've danced as you've been praising,
You've touched My very heart,
But this, your trail-blazing...
Is just the very start!

It's now the time for action!
I urge you to arise!
For you, My army faction,
Can lead the foe's demise!
You need to plan assignments,
And take anointing fire,
To ratify alignments,
That can take My purpose higher.

Arise, I say, be skilful,
My soldiers and My Bride.
Be focused, strong and wilful
As My truths you carry wide.
Arise, I say, with power;
The power of My might,
And take to arms this hour
With My strength, My sword, My light!

Arise! The Jews defender!
Comfort! Pray! Protect!
For I, the Lord am sender....
Of you, My brave elect!
Arise, and look to Zion
As My vanguard and My pride,
And hold to Judah's Lion
For this heav'n-bound, bumpy ride!

Juliet Dawn

"...My vanguard and My pride"

— The End —

Contacts

For e-mail enquiries:
brendataylor94@tiscali.co.uk

For postal enquiries or orders:
Please see website for address details

For telephone enquiries:
07946 456710

To speak to Juliet:
07711 317598

To e-mail Juliet:
jasonandjulie@doolan4240.fsnet.co.uk

Website:
www.dovetail-music.co.uk

To find out what's happening with Israel events:
www.mordecaivoice.co.uk

Resources

Dovetail Music has a wide range of resources available. These include:

POETRY BOOKS
"RAINBOWS AND STORMCLOUDS" by Juliet Dawn
"RISING FROM THE ASHES" by Juliet Dawn
"MATURITY, DESTINY AND FAITH" by Juliet Dawn
These books are challenging, inspiring, and insightful, bringing something unique and prophetic from God's heart. Equally, Juliet shares with you her traumatic journey through grief and brokenness to restoration.

HEALING CD
"HEALING SPRINGS" - Teaching, poetry, songs, blessings.

MUSIC CDs
"HEAVEN'S SONG"
"HIGHER CALL"
These are beautiful and exceptional albums, crafted from the song-writing gift of Brenda Taylor, the production skill of DB Studios (Lincoln) and the vocal richness of Juliet Dawn.
Highly acclaimed and universally popular.

TEACHING CDs
By popular request, the accessible and strategic teachings of Brenda Taylor are now available on CD. These are blessing and informing God's people on a wide scale and as such a diversity of titles are available, please see catalogue (available on request) for full list.

Other music CDs, music books and DVDs are also available. Please see website
www.dovetail-music.co.uk

SISTER BOOKS ALSO AVAILABLE ARE:

"RAINBOWS AND STORMCLOUDS"

Juliet's journey through
trauma and grief.

And "RISING FROM THE ASHES"

Juliet's onward journey from brokenness
to hope and restoration.

ALSO "MATURITY, DESTINY AND FAITH"

Challenging and Insightful: a great book for those
searching for God or looking for inspiration.

NOW ALSO AVAILABLE:

Small booklet of prophetic poetry related to
God's heart and agenda for the Jewish people.

"ISRAEL - GOD'S CHOSEN"